SECOND AND THIRD AMENDMENTS: THE RIGHT TO SECURITY

BY RICH SMITH

SERIES CONSULTANT: SCOTT HARR, J.D. CRIMINAL JUSTICE
DEPARTMENT CHAIR, CONCORDIA UNIVERSITY ST. PAUL

VISIT US AT
WWW.ABDOPUBLISHING.COM

Published by ABDO Publishing Company, 8000 West 78th Street, Suite 310, Edina, MN 55439.
Copyright ©2008 by Abdo Consulting Group, Inc. International copyrights reserved in all countries.
No part of this book may be reproduced in any form without written permission from the publisher.
Abdo & Daughters™ is a trademark and logo of ABDO Publishing Company.

Printed in the United States.

Editor: John Hamilton
Graphic Design: John Hamilton
Cover Design: Neil Klinepier
Cover Illustration: Getty Images
Interior Photos and Illustrations: p 1 Constitution & flag, iStockphoto; p 4 shadow of person holding gun, Getty Images; p 5 gun in drawer, Getty Images; p 7 man at gun show, Corbis; p 8 tank, iStockphoto; p 9 man holding sawed-off shotgun, Corbis; p 10 musket firing, ©2001 John Hamilton; p 11 reenactors firing muskets, ©2001 John Hamilton; p 13 James Brady at Supreme Court, AP Images; p 14 Dred Scott, Corbis; p 15 militiaman charging, AP Images; p 17 hunter in field with shotgun, iStockphoto; p 19 reenactor in Colonial uniform walking past house, Corbis; p 21 Revolutionary War reenactors walk past house in woods, AP Images; p 23 young woman on bed, iStockphoto; p 24 Griswold & Jahncke, Corbis; p 25 Supreme Court, iStockphoto; p 27 abortion protesters, AP Images; p 29 Constitution & gavel, iStockphoto.

Library of Congress Cataloging-in-Publication Data

Smith, Rich, 1954-
  Second and third amendments : the right to security / Rich Smith.
     p. cm. -- (The Bill of Rights)
  Includes index.
  ISBN 978-1-59928-915-1
  1. Firearms--Law and legislation--United States--Juvenile literature. 2. United States. Constitution. 2nd Amendment--Juvenile literature. 3. Requisitions, Military--United States--Juvenile literature. 4. United States. Constitution. 3rd Amendment--Juvenile literature. I. Title.

KF4557.S65 2008
344.7305'33--dc22
                                        2007014572

CONTENTS

THE SECOND AMENDMENT

The U.S. Department of Justice found that nearly 70 percent of all murders, 42 percent of all robberies, and 21 percent of all aggravated assaults reported to police in one recent year involved the use of a gun. The Justice Department also found that a gun was involved more than 400,000 times during that same year in crimes other than murder and suicide.

What do those figures teach us? Guns are bad.

On the other hand, university crime researchers found that an attempted murder, robbery, or aggravated assault was stopped more than 2.5 million times during one recent year by ordinary citizens armed with a gun for self-defense.

Below: Guns can be used to commit crimes—or protect their owners from becoming victims.

The researchers also found that those same citizens 92 percent of the time only had to point their gun at the criminal in order to save the victim from death or other bodily harm.

What do those figures teach us? Guns are good.

Whether you believe guns are dangerous or useful, the fact is that many, many people in America have them. By some estimates there are 250 million guns in the hands of the law-abiding and the law-breaking alike. That's nearly one gun for every adult in the country. No other nation in the world has that many guns compared to its population. One reason for this is that no other nation in the world has the Second Amendment to the U.S. Constitution. The Constitution is a document that describes how the U.S. government is set up and operated. It also explains the job of the president, the lawmakers of Congress, and the people who work as judges.

At the end of the Constitution are 26 additional instructions for the government. These are called amendments. The first 10 make up what is known as the Bill of Rights. The Bill of Rights lists the special freedoms every human is born with and is able to enjoy in America. Also, the Bill of Rights tells the government that it cannot stop people from fully using and enjoying those freedoms unless the government has an extremely good reason for doing so.

The Second Amendment deals with guns. That much everyone can agree on. But what they can't agree on is whether the Second Amendment guarantees individual Americans the right to privately own and carry weapons, or if it gives that right only to groups of Americans organized by the government into a type of army known as a militia.

One thing is certain: The arguments over what the Second Amendment guarantees are among the loudest, longest, and most heated of any involving the Bill of Rights.

Above: Is a loaded handgun kept in a home a menace or a possible life-saving tool?

CHOOSE YOUR WEAPON

Here is what the Second Amendment says: "A well regulated Militia, being necessary to the security of a free State, the right of the people to keep and bear Arms, shall not be infringed."

The "arms" mentioned in the amendment are not the kind that grow out from the upper left and right sides of the human body. The arms the amendment's authors are talking about here are firearms. Guns, in other words.

But who are the authors talking about when they use the word "people"? It's not clear from the way the amendment is written whether they mean people in a militia or people as individuals.

Neither is it clear what kinds of guns the framers of the Second Amendment are talking about. Do they mean pistols and rifles? Or do they also mean machine guns and bazookas? Slingshots and bows-and-arrows? What about cannons? Does the Second Amendment allow you to stick a cannon on top of a car and turn it into a tank? Can a stick of dynamite count as a firearm under the amendment? How about something that explodes in the shape of a mushroom cloud and causes radioactive fallout to rain down from the skies for miles in all directions?

And what kinds of uses for arms did the Second Amendment have in mind? Guns for target practice? Guns for hunting? Guns for personal self-defense? Guns for defense of the country?

What is interesting about these questions is that they were not asked by too many people until the 20th century. Unfortunately, the answers given have not always been as helpful as people might have liked.

Facing page: A gun show in West Palm Beach, Florida. At traveling shows such as this, guns on sale to the general public range from assault rifles to all varieties of handguns and accessories.

Below: Can ordinary U.S. citizens own a tank? The Supreme Court put that question to rest in the case of *United States v. Miller.* The Court ruled that people do not have a right to own unusually dangerous or powerful weapons.

The answers that have come closest to putting Second Amendment debates to rest are those given by the U.S. Supreme Court in the 1939 case of *United States v. Miller.* Here, the High Court explained what a militia is. The justices said a militia is made up mainly of civilians who are expected to defend the country when called on by the government. The Court added that these civilians were supposed to show up for duty with their own guns. However, the guns had to be the kind that most ordinary civilians would likely keep in their homes. That would mean pistols and rifles, since most gun owners do not keep machine guns, bazookas, cannons, and tanks.

The *Miller* case reached the Supreme Court after a man by the name of Jack Miller was arrested for owning a sawed-off shotgun. He broke a law that was created when the U.S. Congress passed the National Firearms Act in 1934. It was a law designed to get machine guns and other extremely powerful weapons out of the hands of gangsters, racketeers, and other criminals who were using them to terrorize entire cities. Sawed-off shotguns were considered dangerous to public safety because they were small enough for a bandit to easily hide one inside his coat. He could bring it inside a bank and no one would know he had the weapon until he pulled it out and ordered the tellers to give him all the money.

Miller did not believe Congress had the authority to make a law like the National Firearms Act.

Miller thought the new law violated the Second Amendment. He believed that his Second Amendment rights allowed him as an individual to own any type of gun he wanted, especially if he might be called to serve in a militia and defend the country. Miller's attorney asked the federal district court to drop all charges in the case. The judge did just that because he agreed with Miller that the National Firearms Act was unconstitutional.

The federal government appealed the judge's decision. The government took the case to the U.S. Supreme Court. This time the ruling went against Miller. Every one of the Supreme Court justices agreed with the government and said that the National Firearms Act did not violate the Second Amendment. They also decided that a sawed-off shotgun is not a weapon that members of a militia would use, and for that reason alone it was proper for the government to pass a law saying that people could not keep and bear sawed-off shotguns and other kinds of unusually dangerous or powerful weapons.

Left: In 1930, criminals used a violin case to hide a sawed-off shotgun during a robbery of the Port Newark National Bank in Newark, New Jersey. The *Miller* case was brought before the Supreme Court to contest the 1934 National Firearms Act, which banned sawed-off shotguns and other powerful weapons to keep them out of the hands of gangsters and other criminals.

REASONS WHY "KEEP AND BEAR ARMS" IS IN THE SECOND AMENDMENT

Above: A close-up view of a musket being fired.

WHY DID THE AUTHORS of the Bill of Rights want to guarantee a right of the people to keep and bear arms? There are two important reasons. First, the Founding Fathers, the authors of the Constitution, did not like the idea of leaving the defense of America only to a full-time, professional army. Many European countries at that time had professional armies, and it often led to problems of many kinds. For one thing, a full-time army cost a lot of money. Also, professional soldiers in the 1700s often grew bored when not fighting wars. They sometimes entertained themselves by bullying ordinary citizens, stealing people's possessions, or even raping women. The Second Amendment's creators thought the answer to those problems was to have armed citizens play an active role in the defense of the country.

The second reason the Constitution's authors wanted to guarantee a right of the people to keep and bear arms was so that the government would not easily become a dictatorship. Many countries of Europe did not allow their citizens to own guns. As a result, those European governments had little fear in trampling their own citizens' liberties.

The "keep and bear arms" wording in the original text of the Second Amendment was a bit different from that which Congress later presented to the states for ratification. An early version went like this: "The right of the people to keep and bear arms shall not be infringed; a well armed and well regulated militia being the best security of a free country; but no person religiously scrupulous of bearing arms shall be compelled to render military service in person."

Another version read this way: "A well regulated militia, composed of the body of the people, being the best security of a free state, the right of the people to keep and bear arms, shall not be infringed, but no one religiously scrupulous of bearing arms, shall be compelled to render military service in person."

The final version was this: "A well regulated Militia, being the security of a free State, the right of the people to keep and bear Arms, shall not be infringed."

Below: Actors portraying Colonial militia reenact the Battle of Newtown, near Elmira, New York.

FIGHTING OVER ITS MEANING

Those who argue that the Second Amendment applies only to militias have pointed to the *Miller* case as proof that they are right. But so have those who argue that the Second Amendment guarantees the right of individuals to keep and bear arms. Each side of the argument has found something in the *Miller* decision to support their viewpoint. That is why the meaning of the Second Amendment has been argued about in more than 200 court cases between 1939 and the present.

One of those cases involved a federal law called the Brady Handgun Violence Prevention Act of 1993. This law required the government to set up a system for checking the backgrounds of people who wanted to buy firearms. Gun buyers first had to fill out a special form. Next, the seller sent the completed form to law enforcement officials, who searched police records and court files to see if the person wanting to buy the gun had a criminal past or was mentally ill. The sale of the gun could only be completed if the buyer turned out to be a law-abiding person with no psychological health problems.

A law enforcement official in Montana did not like certain parts of the Brady Act. He sued the government to have those parts ruled unconstitutional. The case worked its way up to the Supreme Court. In 1997, the Court ruled in favor of the Montana lawman, whose name was Jay Printz. The case was known as *Printz v. United States*.

To help it decide the *Printz* case, the Supreme Court justices looked back through history at earlier rulings on the Second Amendment. That is a very common practice for courts. Looking back at what was decided in the past can show the way to the future.

Facing page: Former White House Press Secretary James Brady is pushed outside the Supreme Court in 1996 after a hearing to discuss the Brady Handgun Violence Prevention Act. The law was named after Brady, who was seriously wounded in the 1981 assassination attempt on President Ronald Reagan.

Above: Dred Scott, the man who lost the 1856 Supreme Court suit that attempted to show that slaves were U.S. citizens.

The first time the Second Amendment came up for discussion in a Supreme Court case was in 1856. The country was only a few short years from bloody civil war over the issue of slavery. And it was a slavery case in which the Second Amendment was involved. The case was *Dred Scott v. Sanford*. It was about whether slaves were in fact citizens of the United States. The Supreme Court said no, they were not. To prove that slaves were not citizens, the court listed all the rights slaves would own if they were citizens. Among those rights were freedom of speech and freedom to "keep and carry arms." Slaves could claim none of those.

The *Dred Scott* decision is considered by historians to be one of the Supreme Court's worst ever because it gave approval for slavery. But it is sometimes pointed to by Second Amendment debaters in support of their positions.

Another interesting case from the 19th century was *Presser v. Illinois*. This Supreme Court case was decided in 1886. It made clear that a militia can legally be formed only by the government. That's not what Herman Presser of Chicago, Illinois, believed when he joined a militia formed by a group of laborers. Their militia was called the Study and Resistance Association. It was organized to defend against armed thugs hired by the owners of the factories where the militia members were employed.

The militia members had been demanding better wages and better working conditions. They held rallies to inspire their coworkers at the factories to stand up to the bosses and go out on strike if necessary to get what they wanted. This made the factory owners very angry. They tried to prevent strikes by frightening the workers. The factory owners did this by unleashing on them the hired thugs. The thugs showed up at the workers' strike-planning meetings and hit them with clubs, smashed their furniture, and warned them to get back to work or face worse treatment next time.

The militia that Presser had joined to defend against the thugs practiced marching with guns and held parades to show off their military skills. The state of Illinois took notice of the Study and Resistance Association and in 1879 charged its members with belonging to an unlawful militia. Presser asked the courts to dismiss the case against him.

The Supreme Court had the last word. For Presser, that last word was not good. A lower court had found him guilty and the Supreme Court allowed that verdict to stand.

Below: A militia member practices assault tactics during a training session in northern Idaho in 1995. Small, armed militias such as this are usually illegal.

DOES NOT APPLY TO THE STATES

One Second Amendment argument that seems to have come to an end is the one about whether the Second Amendment applies to federal, state, and local governments. High Court rulings over the years have made clear that the Second Amendment applies only to the federal government and not to the states.

That means states and cities are free to make up just about any law they want about guns. They can pass laws requiring people who seek to own a gun to wait days or weeks after buying it before they can take the weapon home from the store. Or they can pass laws making it illegal to own guns that load with too many bullets, or fire bullets at too fast a rate. They even can make a law requiring every adult to own and keep a gun in the house in case a militia needs to be called up.

The Second Amendment is only one of a few that do not apply to the states. Amendments that apply to the states are called incorporated amendments. In the 1968 case of *Duncan v. Louisiana*, the Supreme Court ruled that an amendment can be applied to the states if the freedom it guarantees is basic to the American concept of justice. Gun ownership is not considered by the courts to be basic to the American concept of justice.

Not everyone would agree with that. Some would argue that gun ownership is as basic to American justice as it gets. Others will argue the opposite. Whatever else, don't expect the debates over the Second Amendment to go away any time soon.

Facing page:
The Second Amendment applies only to the federal government, which means the states are free to pass their own firearm laws, including rules for ownership of guns used for hunting.

THE THIRD AMENDMENT

In a way, the Third Amendment is related to the Second Amendment. It too deals with people who bear arms, but not people who belong to militias. Instead, the people are soldiers, those who belong to the U.S. Army.

The Third Amendment also is about another group of people who are not soldiers. They are people who own homes.

The idea behind the Third Amendment is that a person's home is his or her castle. As a result, the owner of that home cannot be forced to roll out the welcome mat for soldiers who have no place to live.

Soldiers usually live in army camps or forts or on huge military bases. Housing is provided for them there by the government. Sometimes the government doesn't have enough housing for all of its soldiers. The Bill of Rights was written at a time when it was common for governments to force homeowners to let soldiers live with them. The homeowners also had to buy food for the soldiers and clean up after them.

The Third Amendment guarantees homeowners the right to say no to the government when it wants to turn a home into an army barracks. However, the Third Amendment is not an absolute right. There are situations when the government can still force homeowners to let soldiers live with them. But this can only happen if the government has an extremely good reason.

Facing page: A reenactor dressed as a Colonial soldier walks past a home with a Christmas decoration over the doorway in historic Colonial Williamsburg, Virginia. The Third Amendment gives homeowners the right to say no, in times of peace, if the government wants to turn their homes into barracks for soldiers.

A HOME IS A CASTLE, NOT A BARRACKS

THE THIRD AMENDMENT was written to prevent the newly created government of the United States from passing laws like those the English Parliament came up with when America was still under British rule. Those laws were called the Quartering Acts. There were two of them. The first was approved by Parliament in 1765. The second was approved in 1774.

The Quartering Act of 1765 was not quite as bad as the one that came nine years later. This first one said that British soldiers were to be housed in barracks. Barracks are buildings specially made for an army. A single barrack is big enough to shelter dozens of soldiers at a time. But if there were not enough barracks for all the soldiers stationed in a town, the Quartering Act of 1765 allowed those who would be stuck outside to be moved into inns, barns, and empty houses. The law also made it the duty of the owners of those places to provide at their own expense all the food, bedding, and other necessities the quartered soldiers needed.

Then came the Quartering Act of 1774. This was part of a collection of harsh laws meant to break the will of the colonists to resist British authority. The new Quartering Act required everything the older Quartering Act required. But this time the list of places where soldiers could be housed was lengthened to include private homes that families were living in. The colonists were very angry about this. So great was their anger that it helped fan the fires leading up to America's declaration of independence from Britain in 1776.

Facing page: Revolutionary War reenactors march past a Colonial-era house near Washington Crossing, Pennsylvania, on December 25, 2003, during the 51ˢᵗ annual reenactment of George Washington's Christmas crossing of the Delaware River in 1776. The Quartering Act of 1774, which ordered owners of private homes to house and feed British soldiers, was one of the unfair laws that led the colonists to declare independence from England. The Third Amendment to the U.S. Constitution was designed to stop the government from quartering soldiers in private homes during peacetime.

A Right to Bedroom Privacy

The text of the Third Amendment reads: "No Soldier shall, in time of peace be quartered in any house, without the consent of the Owner, nor in time of war, but in a manner to be prescribed by law."

Today, hardly anybody talks about the Third Amendment as guaranteeing the freedom of homeowners to refuse housing soldiers in their homes. The reason is that the quartering of soldiers in private residences has not happened in any big way since the last time a war was fully fought on American soil. That was the Civil War in the early 1860s. But there has been plenty of talk about the Third Amendment for reasons having little to do with where soldiers sleep. It turns out that the Third Amendment also guarantees civilians privacy in the bedroom.

In 1965 the U.S. Supreme Court gave a ruling on the case of *Griswold v. Connecticut.* The High Court found that an 1879 Connecticut law making it illegal for married couples to use birth control was unconstitutional because it violated the right to bedroom privacy.

The state of Connecticut had been sued over this law twice before. Both times the courts threw out the case because the plaintiffs did not actually have a valid reason for suing. For example, in one case the plaintiff was a doctor who sued because his patients could not purchase condoms and other birth control devices. The Court told him he was not allowed to sue because he was not the one harmed by the law. The Court said that only people who wanted to use birth control or who wanted to sell birth control products to others could sue since the law affected just them.

Facing page: Over the years, the Supreme Court has decided that the Third Amendment contains an implied right to privacy.

Above: Estelle Griswold (left), director of the Planned Parenthood Clinic in New Haven, Connecticut, and Cornelia Jahncke (right), president of the Parenthood League of Connecticut, flash a victory sign after the Supreme Court ruled that the state's birth control law was unconstitutional.

The odd thing about this law was that it had rarely ever been used against anyone in the 80 or so years between the time it was enacted and the time that a woman by the name of Estelle Griswold was arrested for breaking it. Griswold ran a Planned Parenthood clinic in the city of New Haven, Connecticut. She opened the clinic for the purpose of putting the Connecticut law to the test. Griswold's plan was to be arrested so she could then sue to have the law struck down.

After her arrest, Griswold was put on trial and was found guilty. She then appealed that verdict by saying her federally guaranteed privacy rights had been violated. The case went first to a state appeals court and then to the Connecticut Supreme Court. Both those courts ruled against Griswold. They said there is no right to privacy written into the Constitution.

She next took her case to the U.S. Supreme Court. A majority of the justices agreed with the lower courts that the right to privacy was not mentioned by name in the Constitution. But then they added that this didn't matter. They said the right

to privacy was hinted at by the existence of several other actual rights. The Third Amendment right against soldiers quartering in private homes was one of those. The result of the Supreme Court's decision in the *Griswold* case was to make it legal for married couples in Connecticut and all other states in the country to use birth control.

Above: The front of the U.S. Supreme Court building in Washington, D.C.

MAKING ABORTION LEGAL

The concept of a right to privacy hidden within the Third Amendment, and other amendments, was again referred to by the Supreme Court when it decided the 1972 case of *Eisenstadt v. Baird*. This was a case that came out of Massachusetts, which had a birth-control law much like Connecticut's, but the Massachusetts law applied specifically to unmarried couples. Guided by its *Griswold* ruling, the Supreme Court ruled in the *Eisenstadt* case that all birth control decisions should be private matters.

In 1973, both the *Griswold* and *Eisenstadt* rulings played a role in helping the Supreme Court decide the case of *Roe v. Wade*. This case made it legal for women in all 50 states to obtain an abortion. The "Roe" of *Roe v. Wade* was a Texas woman whose real name was Norma Jean McCorvey. In court papers, she was called Jane Roe to protect her identity. McCorvey said she had been raped and became pregnant as a result of that attack. She wanted to end that unwanted pregnancy, but abortions in Texas were illegal. Two attorneys came to McCorvey's aid in 1970 and filed suit on her behalf to have Texas's abortion law thrown out.

The U.S. Supreme Court decided two things in *Roe v. Wade*. First, it found that the Texas law against abortion was unclearly written. In order for a law to be constitutional it must be clear about what is allowed and what is not allowed. That was strike one against the Texas abortion law. Second, the Supreme Court said that the right to privacy allows women to decide whether or not they want to have a baby. The *Griswold* and *Eisenstadt* cases had made clear that the government could not prevent couples from using birth control. Since they could not be stopped from using birth control, then they also could not be stopped from choosing an abortion, because abortion is a form of birth control. That was strike two and three against the Texas abortion law.

Facing page: People for and against *Roe v. Wade* protest in front of the U.S. Supreme Court building in Washington, D.C.

A First for the Third Amendment

Of course, birth control was not what inspired the authors of the Bill of Rights to craft the Third Amendment. But in all the history of the United States, only once has a lawsuit involving the actual quartering of soldiers reached a federal court of appeals. That happened in 1982, nearly 200 years after the Third Amendment was added to the Constitution.

The case was *Engblom v. Carey*. It was decided by the Second Circuit U.S. Court of Appeals. It did not go any higher than that. In 1979, prison guards at New York's Mid-Orange Correctional Facility went on strike. Some of the striking guards lived at the prison in homes provided by the state government. The governor of New York responded to the strike by ordering soldiers from the National Guard to take the places of the prison guards who had walked off the job. The National Guardsmen had no place to stay during the time they were at the prison. The government told the strikers to immediately move out of the houses provided by the government in order to make room for the soldiers.

Two of the strikers fought back by suing the state of New York and Governor Hugh Carey. The guards who sued were Marianne E. Engblom and Charles E. Palmer. They claimed that New York had abused their Third Amendment rights by giving their homes to the soldiers. The district court where their lawsuit was first filed threw out their case. That court said Engblom and Palmer did not own their homes and because of that they could not sue. The court also pointed out that the homes were owned by the government.

Engblom and Palmer took their case to the appeals court, which later ruled that the Third Amendment did not apply just to homeowners, but also to tenants like Engblom and Palmer.

The appeals court then told the lower court to let the Engblom and Palmer lawsuit go forward. In the end, the two strikers lost. The judge decided they had failed to prove that the government knew it was acting illegally when it ordered Engblom and Palmer out of their homes.

It might be a long time before there ever is another Third Amendment lawsuit. Until then, the Third Amendment will continue to be one of the least-talked-about freedoms listed in the Bill of Rights.

Below: The U.S. Constitution and the Bill of Rights form a basic framework of laws that are constantly reinterpreted to fit the needs of present society.

GLOSSARY

AMENDMENT

When it was created, the Constitution wasn't perfect. The Founding Fathers wisely added a special section. It allowed the Constitution to be changed by future generations. This makes the Constitution flexible. It is able to bend to the will of the people it governs. Changes to the Constitution are called amendments. The first 10 amendments are called the Bill of Rights. An amendment must be approved by two-thirds of both houses of Congress. Once that happens, the amendment must be approved by three-fourths of the states. Then it becomes law. This is a very difficult thing to do. The framers of the Constitution didn't want it changed unless there was a good reason. There have been over 9,000 amendments proposed. Only 27 of them have been ratified, or made into law. Some amendments changed the way our government works. The Twelfth Amendment changed the way we elect our president. The Twenty-Second Amendment limits a president to two terms in office. Constitutional amendments have also increased the freedoms of our citizens. The Thirteenth Amendment finally got rid of slavery. And the Nineteenth Amendment gave women the right to vote.

DEPARTMENT OF JUSTICE, U.S.

A department of the United States government that was created to make sure all U.S. citizens receive fair and impartial justice. The head of the Department of Justice is the United States Attorney General, a member of the president's cabinet. The Department of Justice is also involved in law enforcement. Some of the agencies within the department include the Bureau of Alcohol, Tobacco, and Firearms (ATF), the Federal Bureau of Investigation (FBI), and the Drug Enforcement Administration (DEA).

DICTATORSHIP

A country with a single leader who rules with total power. Citizens of a dictatorship have little or no say in how their country is run. Dictators usually gain their position, and keep their powers, through the use of military force. The Constitution was written to avoid dictatorships. It splits government into three distinct parts: the presidency, Congress, and the Supreme Court. This separation of power keeps any one individual from becoming a dictator.

Founding Fathers

The men who participated in the Constitutional Convention in 1787, especially the ones who signed the Constitution. Some of the Founding Fathers included George Washington, Benjamin Franklin, John Rutledge, Gouverneur Morris, Alexander Hamilton, and James Madison.

High Court

Another name for the United States Supreme Court.

Lawsuit

A legal way to settle a dispute in which both sides argue their case in front of a judge or jury in a court of law. The person who has been wronged is called the plaintiff. The person being sued is called the defendant. Plaintiffs and defendants can be individuals, or they can be businesses or government entities, such as corporations or towns. People can even sue the United States, which is how many cases are filed involving the Constitution and violation of rights.

Ratification

The process of making a proposed law or treaty officially valid. Constitutional amendments are ratified when they are approved by two-thirds of both houses of Congress, and by three-fourths of the states.

Sue

To bring a lawsuit against a person or institution in a court of law.

Supreme Court

The United States Supreme Court is the highest court in the country. There are nine judges on the Supreme Court. They make sure local, state, and federal governments are following the rules spelled out in the United States Constitution. Our understanding of the Constitution evolves over time. It is up to the Supreme Court to decide how the Constitution is applied to today's society. When the Supreme Court rules on a case, other courts in the country must follow the decision in similar situations. In this way, the laws of the Constitution are applied equally to all Americans.

INDEX